This book belongs to

_____

This book is dedicated to my children - Mikey, Kobe, and Jojo.

Copyright © 2024 Grow Grit Press LLC. All rights reserved. No part of this book may be reproduced in any form without permission in writing from the publisher. Please send bulk order requests to info@ninjalifehacks.tv

Paperback ISBN: 978-1-63731-878-2
Hardcover ISBN: 978-1-63731-880-5
eBook ISBN: 978-1-63731-879-9

Printed and bound in the USA.
NinjaLifeHacks.tv

Ninja Life Hacks®
by Mary Nhin

# Honest Ninja

A Children's Book About Why Honesty is the Best Policy

Ninja Life Hacks
by Mary Nhin

One sunny morning, I woke up feeling excited about the big adventure Positive Ninja had planned for us! I had shared with my friend how I struggled with telling little lies and exaggerating, and she told me she had the perfect solution. Best of all, she was going to share it with me!

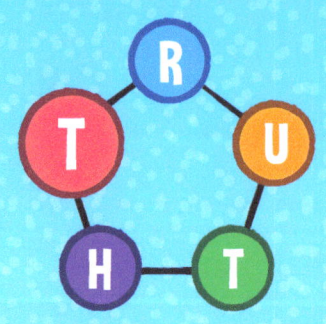

Instead of being upset, I remembered '**T** for **Tell the truth**.'

It's hard for me to tell you this, Dishonest Ninja, but this toy is mine. I lost it.

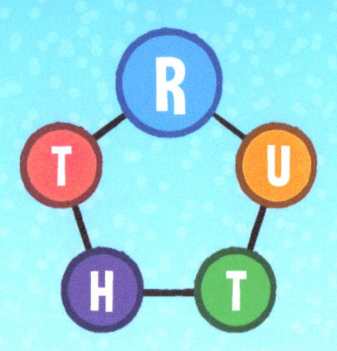

R stands for **Respect** others. That means treating everyone kindly, just like you want to be treated.

U stands for **Understand** others feelings. It's important to listen and understand how others feel, even if they don't say it out loud.

H stands for **Honesty** in all things we do. It means being truthful even when nobody's watching.

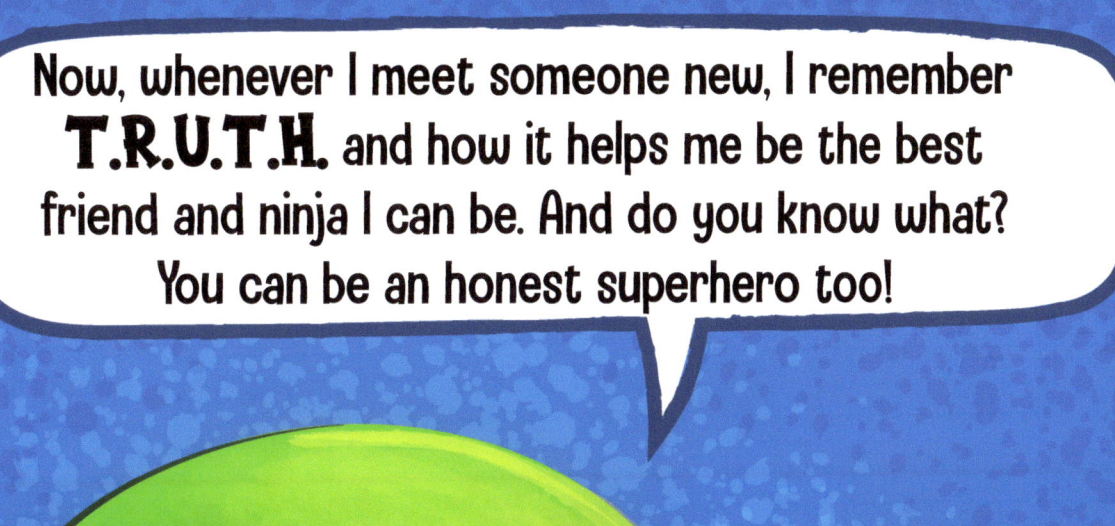

# The path of T.R.U.T.H.

www.ingramcontent.com/pod-product-compliance
Lightning Source LLC
Chambersburg PA
CBHW041521070526
44585CB00002B/39